Exploring Space

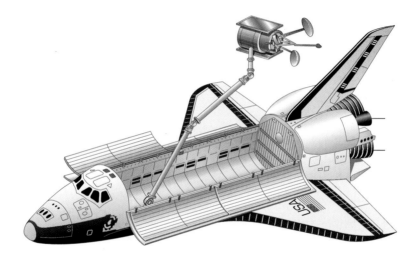

Elizabeth Miles

OXFORD
UNIVERSITY PRESS

Great Clarendon Street, Oxford OX2 6DP

Oxford University Press is a department of the University of Oxford.
It furthers the University's objective of excellence in research,
scholarship, and education by publishing worldwide in

Oxford New York

Auckland Bangkok Buenos Aires Cape Town Chennai
Dar es Salaam Delhi Hong Kong Istanbul Karachi Kolkata
Kuala Lumpur Madrid Melbourne Mexico City Mumbai
Nairobi São Paulo Shanghai Taipei Tokyo Toronto

Oxford is a registered trade mark of Oxford University Press
in the UK and in certain other countries

Text © Elizabeth Miles 2002

British Library Cataloguing in Publication Data

Data available

ISBN 0 19 917456 3

Also available as packs

The Earth in Space Inspection Pack (one of each book)
ISBN 0 19 917458 X

The Earth in Space Class Pack (six of each book)
ISBN 0 19 917459 8

10 9 8 7 6 5 4 3 2

Designed by Alicia Howard at Tangerine Tiger

Printed in Hong Kong

Acknowledgements

The Publisher would like to thank the following for permission to reproduce photographs:

Associated Press/Steve Helber: p 16; Associated Press/Lockheed: p 28 (top); Associated
Press/NASA: pp 12, 13 (top left), 15 (bottom), 24 (bottom), 25 (bottom left)); Associated
Press/Lynne Sladky: p 26 (left); Corbis UK Ltd: p 8 (top); Corbis UK Ltd/Bettmann: p 6
(bottom); Corbis UK Ltd/Hulton Deutsch Collection: p 5 (bottom left); Corbis UK Ltd/
Archivo Iconografico S.A.: p 5 (top); Corbis UK Ltd/London Aerial Photo Library: p 5
(bottom right); Corbis UK Ltd/Roger Ressmeyer: pp 4 (background), 6 (top), 13 (bottom),
22 (top), 25 (bottom right); European Space Agency: p 19; Hulton Getty: p 8 (bottom);
Hulton Getty/NASA: p 21 (top); NASA: pp 9 (left), 11, 13 (top right), 14 (both), 15 (top),
20 (both) 24/25 (top), 26 (bottom right), 27 (both), 28 (bottom), 29 (both); PA PicSelect:
p17 (both); Photodisc: pp 22 (bottom), 30; Science Photo Library/NASA: pp 9 (right), 18,
21 (bottom)

Front cover: NASA/Roger Ressmeyer/Corbis UK Ltd

Back cover: NASA

Illustrations are by: Stefan Chabluk, Richard Morris, David Russell, Thomas Sperling
and Colin Sullivan

Contents

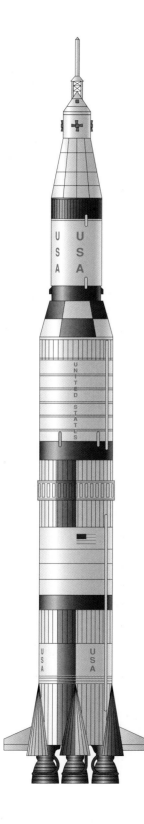

Looking into space

The shining **stars** and **planets** in the night sky, and the Sun and **Moon**, have fascinated the human race for thousands of years. Ancient civilizations believed that the Sun and Moon were gods. The Ancient Greeks believed that stars formed pictures of mythical gods, heroes, and animals.

It took many centuries for astronomers to discover the truth about our Solar System, to learn that the Earth was round and not flat, and to work out the position of the Earth in relation to its neighbouring planets. Later, with the invention of the telescope, astronomers were able to uncover even more.

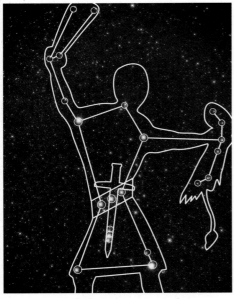

▲ In the night sky of the Northern Hemisphere, you can see the star formations that the Ancient Greeks used to imagine were pictures in the sky. For example, three stars mark out a belt worn by Orion, the hunter.

The first astronomers

Ptolemy (AD 100–170)
The Egyptian astronomer, Claudius Ptolemy, worked out a theory that the Earth was at the centre of the **Universe**, with the Sun, Moon, and stars revolving around it.

Copernicus (1473–1543)
The Polish priest and astronomer, Nicolaus Copernicus, claimed that the Earth, along with other planets, moved around the Sun.

Amazing discoveries

Before the 17th century, all observations of outer space had been made with just the naked eye. But in 1609, the Italian scientist Galileo Galilei (1564–1642) became the first person to use a telescope to study the sky. He saw craters on the Moon, rings around Saturn, and discovered four moons **orbiting** Jupiter!

Galileo used a **refractor** telescope, but in 1668, the English scientist Isaac Newton made a more powerful type of telescope, called a **reflector** telescope. In 1781, astronomers William and Catherine Herschel were the first to find a new planet through a telescope – it was Uranus, the seventh planet from the Sun in our Solar System.

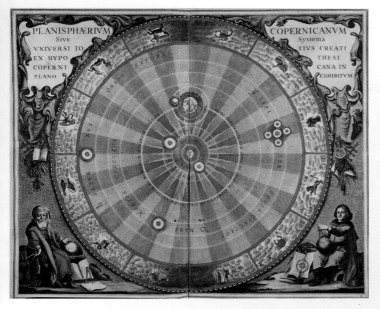

▲ Copernicus' view of the Solar System. Only six planets appear in it because at the time no one knew that Uranus, Neptune, or Pluto existed.

Brahe (1546–1601)

Tycho Brahe, a Danish astronomer, took lots of accurate measurements of how the planets change position. These observations led to a completely different view of the Solar System.

Kepler (1571–1630)

After Brahe's death, his assistant, a German astronomer, Johannes Kepler, looked at Brahe's measurements and used them to prove that each planet orbits the Sun, following an oval path called an ellipse.

▼ William Herschel was a German musician who became a telescope-maker. He completed this telescope in 1789.

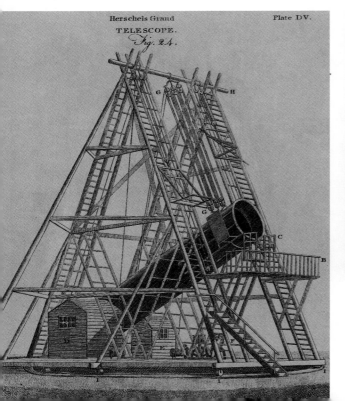

▲ Many telescopes today are radio telescopes. They pick up radio waves from space. The Lovell telescope, built in 1957 with a 76 m dish, was the first giant radio telescope.

Rocket power

When we consider space exploration today, we don't think of just telescopes – we think of spacecraft and astronauts, too. But before spacecraft and their crew could be launched, rocket power had to be developed. This very powerful force was necessary to boost **satellites** and other heavy equipment into space.

Small beginnings

AD 1000

The first "rockets" were made in China about a thousand years ago. They were arrows powered by gunpowder, just like fireworks, and were used for shooting at the enemy.

1903

In 1903, a Russian master of rocket science, Konstantin Tsiolkovsky, published the first practical ideas on how to use a rocket to travel into space.

1926

In 1926, an American called Robert Goddard launched the first liquid-fuelled rocket. It only stayed up for 2.5 seconds. Later, another of his rockets gained a world altitude record, reaching a height of 3 km.

1950

During the Second World War (1939–1945), the German *V-2* rocket was developed as a missile to attack enemy targets. After the war, the German *V-2* engineer, Wernher von Braun, went to the USA to develop it as a space rocket. The first launch was in 1950, from Cape Canaveral in Florida.

◀ Robert Goddard with his first liquid-fuelled rocket, launched in 1926 at Massachusetts, USA

V-2

◀ *Saturn V*, which took men to the **Moon**, was the biggest rocket ever – with the *Apollo* spacecraft on top it was 110.6 m high.

Saturn V

1957

In 1957, Russian scientists successfully used their *A1* rocket to launch a satellite into space. The *Sputnik 1* satellite orbited the Earth for almost three months. The success of the *A1* rocket marked the beginning of the Space Age. Later, in 1961, a similar rocket (the *Vostok*) was used to launch the first person into **orbit**.

Vostok

How a rocket works

To escape the pull of the Earth's **gravity**, a rocket must travel at 40,000 kph (about twenty times the speed of the supersonic aircraft *Concorde*). How can a rocket reach such a speed?

Rockets burn a lot of fuel. The fuel is burnt in a "combustion chamber". Liquid fuel, such as hydrogen, is fed into the chamber from one tank, while liquid oxygen is fed from another tank. Once mixed with oxygen, the fuel will burn when ignited and create gas which expands very fast, creating enormous pressure. The gas is directed downwards through a nozzle which pushes the rocket up at high speed.

To enable them to travel up into space, rockets are built in several sections, called stages. Each stage holds its own fuel. As the fuel is burnt up in each stage, that stage falls away, making the rest of the rocket lighter, so that it is able to continue on its way.

▼ A rocket engine

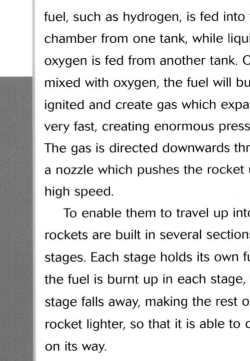

liquid oxygen tank

liquid hydrogen tank

igniter

combustion chamber

nozzle

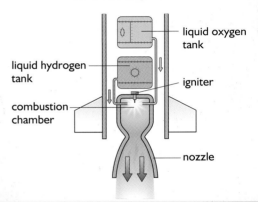

The first explorers

The Space Age began with the launch of *Sputnik 1* on 4 October 1957. Throughout the years that followed, many brave astronauts achieved record-breaking flights into space.

Space firsts

1957, Laika

The first living thing to be launched into space to **orbit** the Earth was not a person at all. Laika was a Russian dog. Laika's spaceship did not return to Earth and after seven days she was given an automatic injection which killed her, so that she did not have to suffer.

1961, Yuri Gagarin

The first human being in space was Yuri Gagarin. The 27-year-old Russian orbited the Earth in a mission that lasted 108 minutes.

Gagarin's safe landing

Gagarin flew in *Vostok 1* (see below). At the end of the mission, the descent **capsule** separated from the instrument module. The landing was unusual. Instead of landing in the spacecraft, Gagarin was strapped into an ejector seat that shot out of the capsule as it fell to Earth. A parachute attached to Gagarin opened and the cosmonaut floated, slowly and safely, down to land.

▲ This Russian postage stamp shows Laika and the *Sputnik* satellite that sent her into space.

▶ *Vostok 1*

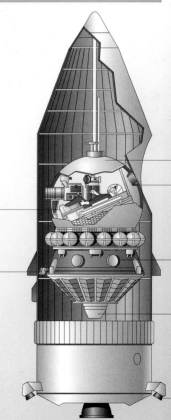

The ejector seat held emergency food, water, and a dinghy in case it landed in the sea.

fine control rocket (these rockets were used to change the direction the spacecraft flew in)

1963, **Valentina Tereshkova**

The first woman in space was a 26-year-old Russian called Valentina Tereshkova. During her three-day mission in *Vostok 6*, she travelled round the Earth 48 times.

1965, **Alexei Leonov**

Russian cosmonaut, Alexei Leonov, was the first person to "walk" in space. The 30-year-old was attached to his spacecraft by a line so that he did not float away. He spent nearly 25 minutes floating in space while he and the spacecraft orbited Earth.

1969, **Neil Armstrong**

American astronaut Neil Armstrong became the first person to set foot on the **Moon** (see pages 12 – 13).

Vostok's descent capsule

hatch

The instrument module was controlled by scientists on Earth.

The retro-rocket brought the capsule out of orbit.

fine control rocket

G-force

Before humans could be sent into space, tests were needed to make sure they would be safe. For example, the effects of **G-forces** of six, or more, during launch and re-entry had to be tested. (A force of 6-G is six times more than the pull of the Earth's **gravity**.)

▲ This man was shot down a track at high speed. The pressure of the G-force pushed his whole body, including his skin, backwards.

Race to the Moon

By the 1960s, two powerful governments – in the USA and the Soviet Union – each felt they had to be the first to get an astronaut on the **Moon**. They wanted to test the limits of their technology and to explore this mysterious rocky world. The USA developed the *Apollo* spacecraft to do the job.

Apollo spacecraft

The *Apollo* spacecraft had three main parts: the command **module**, service module, and lunar module. During lift-off, the three astronauts sat in the command module, where the controls were.

The service module contained fuel and supplies. Once the *Saturn V* rocket stages had been jettisoned, engines on the service module were used to change the direction of the command module.

The lunar module had its own controls, engines, and fuel, and so could be flown as a separate spacecraft. It was used to take the astronauts down to the Moon's surface. The top part of the lunar module was called the ascent stage. When the astronauts left the Moon, they took off in just this top section. The rest of the module was left behind.

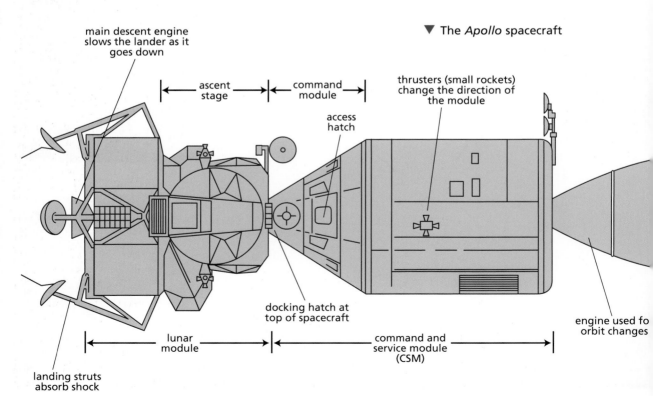

main descent engine slows the lander as it goes down

ascent stage

command module

access hatch

▼ The *Apollo* spacecraft

thrusters (small rockets) change the direction of the module

docking hatch at top of spacecraft

lunar module

command and service module (CSM)

engine used for orbit changes

landing struts absorb shock

Apollo flight profile

An *Apollo* mission to the Moon had to be carefully planned. Mission control watched every stage, ready to deal with any problems.

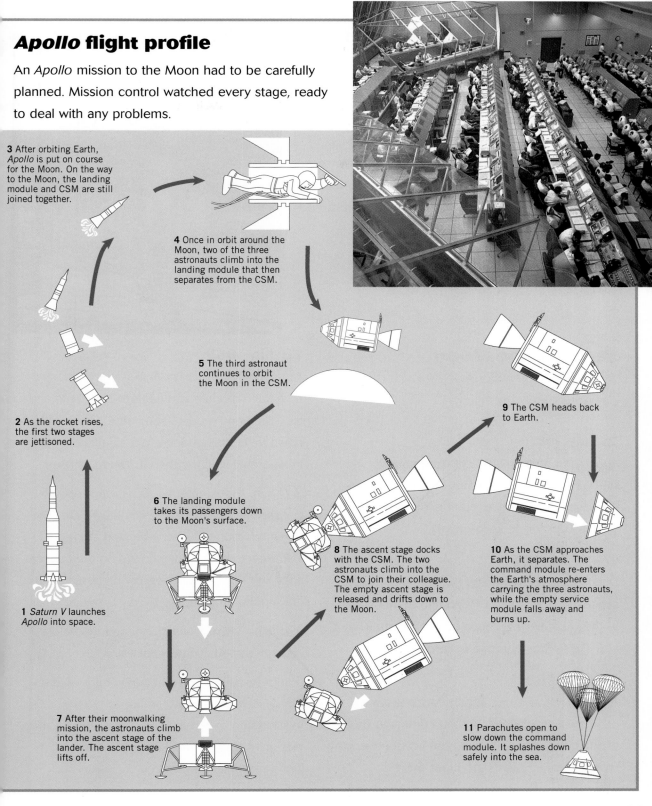

3 After orbiting Earth, *Apollo* is put on course for the Moon. On the way to the Moon, the landing module and CSM are still joined together.

4 Once in orbit around the Moon, two of the three astronauts climb into the landing module that then separates from the CSM.

5 The third astronaut continues to orbit the Moon in the CSM.

9 The CSM heads back to Earth.

2 As the rocket rises, the first two stages are jettisoned.

6 The landing module takes its passengers down to the Moon's surface.

8 The ascent stage docks with the CSM. The two astronauts climb into the CSM to join their colleague. The empty ascent stage is released and drifts down to the Moon.

10 As the CSM approaches Earth, it separates. The command module re-enters the Earth's atmosphere carrying the three astronauts, while the empty service module falls away and burns up.

1 *Saturn V* launches *Apollo* into space.

7 After their moonwalking mission, the astronauts climb into the ascent stage of the lander. The ascent stage lifts off.

11 Parachutes open to slow down the command module. It splashes down safely into the sea.

Moon landing

On 16 July 1969, millions of people turned on their television sets to watch the start of an historic space mission – the launch of *Apollo 11*. Three well-trained astronauts, Neil Armstrong, Buzz Aldrin, and Mike Collins, were on board. Their dangerous mission was to make the first crewed **Moon** landing.

Steps to the Moon
16–20 July 1969

16 July 1969

Apollo 11 began its 403,913-km journey to the Moon. The astronauts had their first meal in space. They experienced headaches as their bodies adjusted to **zero-gravity**.

17–18 July 1969

Duties included re-setting the course of the spaceship towards the Moon and demonstrating to the vast television audiences on Earth what it was like to move around in zero-gravity.

19 July 1969

As *Apollo 11* approached the Moon, a retro-rocket was fired which put the command **module** (holding the astronauts) and the attached landing module, called *Eagle*, into **lunar orbit**.

20 July 1969

Armstrong and Aldrin climbed from the command module into *Eagle*. Next, *Eagle* and the command module separated. *Eagle* drifted down towards the Moon to a safe landing site in an area called the Sea of Tranquility.

3.17 p.m. (Houston time) Armstrong reported to mission control, "Tranquility Base here. The *Eagle* has landed". After checking the module's instruments, the astronauts put on their space suits and made the necessary preparations for leaving the module.

9.45 p.m. The astronauts opened the hatch and Armstrong climbed out.

9.56 p.m. Armstrong placed his right boot on the dusty lunar surface and reported to mission control, "That's one small step for man, one giant leap for mankind". A fifth of the world's population watched on television.

first steps on the Moon

Armstrong says: one giant leap for mankind

Moon rovers

During later missions, astronauts spent as long as 20 hours walking on the Moon's surface, returning to their landing module several times.

▲ The astronauts on *Apollos 15, 16* and *17* used a Lunar Roving Vehicle to travel and take equipment around the Moon's surface.

Moon walk

No one knew what it would be like to walk on the Moon. Luckily, the surface was firm and safe and Armstrong and Aldrin found it easy to move along, in bouncing steps. First, they collected rock and soil samples. Next, they stood the American flag in the ground and spoke to the US President, who congratulated them from his office in the White House. Then the astronauts set up scientific equipment, including a **seismometer** that would pick up "moonquakes". Finally, after their two-and-a-half-hour walk, they returned to *Eagle*, ready for their journey home.

◀ Two thousand rock and soil samples were collected on the *Apollo* missions. Some rocks hold clues as to what the Moon was like in the past. Volcanic rocks show that hot lava once oozed up from beneath the surface of the Moon.

13

Space shuttle

▲ Models of the shuttle were tested in special wind tunnels, to check the shuttle's reactions at top speed.

For every *Apollo* mission, a 2900-tonne rocket (*Saturn V*) had to be built to launch the spacecraft. Each of these rockets and other launch vehicles could only be used once, so they were very expensive. Both the USA and the Soviet Union developed re-usable launch vehicles, called shuttles, so that the increasing number of space missions into Earth's **orbit** would be cheaper.

The American space shuttle was first flown in 1981 and Russia followed with its own similar shuttle in 1988.

Take-off

The American shuttle has its own rocket engines, but its launch is helped by two solid-fuel rocket boosters (SRBs). At an altitude of 50 km, these fall away and land in the sea. They can be retrieved and used again, saving more than $39 million per mission. The giant external fuel tank (ET) falls away next, having fed the shuttle's engines with fuel for nine minutes. It burns up in the Earth's **atmosphere** and is the only part that cannot be used again. Next, the Orbital Manoeuvring System (OMS) engines take over and the shuttle flies onward, orbiting the Earth at a speed of 27,000 km per hour.

The *Challenger* shuttle at lift-off ▶

Landing

To land, the shuttle's OMS engines are fired to slow the shuttle down. As it re-enters the atmosphere, the shuttle's speed falls to 348 km per hour. An outer coating of 32,000 special tiles protect the craft from the heat that builds up as it passes through the atmosphere. The shuttle lands like an aeroplane, intact and re-usable.

▼ The *Discovery* shuttle touches down

▼ Astronauts from the *Endeavour* shuttle repaired the *Hubble Space Telescope*. They wore backpacks containing air and power supplies. Small hand-controlled jets on the backpacks allowed the astronauts to move around in space.

Mission accomplished!

Why send shuttles into space? A shuttle is launched into orbit to carry out essential jobs. Its 18 m-long cargo bay can carry and set up **satellites** in space.

Shuttles have also been sent to repair satellites. In 1993, shuttle astronauts corrected a mirror on the *Hubble Space Telescope*. This orbiting satellite cost $2.1 billion to build, but, at first, it failed to work. Later, there were several other missions to service the telescope.

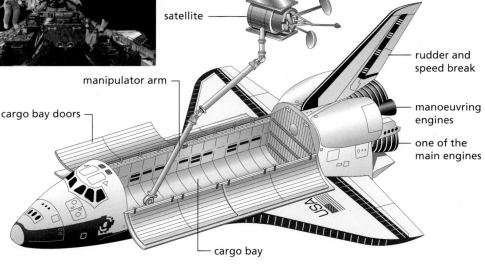

satellite

rudder and speed break

manipulator arm

manoeuvring engines

cargo bay doors

one of the main engines

cargo bay

USA

▲ Shuttles are also now being used to help build the *International Space Station* (see page 25).

Is it worth it?

On 28 January 1986, the *Challenger* space shuttle was launched – it was hoped to be the start of another exciting mission. But after only 73 seconds in the air, the shuttle exploded, killing the seven crew members. The disaster made many people think again about space flight. Was it worth putting people's lives at risk? Should all space missions be stopped? Was money being wasted on space exploration?

Two-and-a-half years later, after the disaster was thoroughly investigated, the space shuttle programme continued. Here are two very different views on the subject.

THE HERALD
Crew die in shuttle disaster

▲ *Challenger* exploded because of a combination of cold weather conditions and a faulty joint design on the boosters. People were shocked to learn that a problem with the seals on the joints had been reported previously, but nothing had been done to avoid risking an accident.

Stop wasting lives and money!

✳ No space mission can be guaranteed safe, so lives should not be put at risk. The launch of a spacecraft only adds to the pollution of our **planet** and uses up more of its limited resources. At lift-off, a shuttle's engines guzzle 290,000 litres of liquid hydrogen and liquid oxygen every minute!

✳ Space missions are a waste of money. The costs are enormous. For example, the *Skylab* space station, launched in the 1970s, cost $2.5 billion, but was abandoned only six years after its launch! Surely, money such as this should be spent on people instead. $2.5 billion would feed and care for ten million starving children for six months – children who might otherwise be among the 40 million people who die of hunger each year.

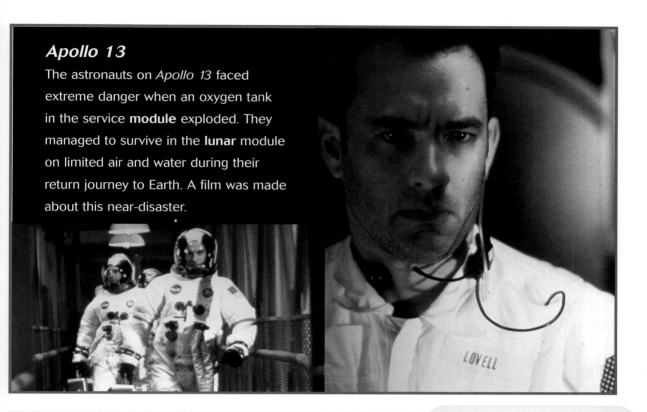

Apollo 13

The astronauts on *Apollo 13* faced extreme danger when an oxygen tank in the service **module** exploded. They managed to survive in the **lunar** module on limited air and water during their return journey to Earth. A film was made about this near-disaster.

✳ We need space flights to put **satellites** into **orbit**, and to repair them. Imagine a world without satellites – we need them for the Internet, international telephone calls, TV transmissions, and navigation systems.

✳ The whole world, rich and poor, could benefit from experiments being carried out in space. They could lead to new medicines and cheaper ways of making important items. Crewed missions or space probes might one day discover valuable resources that we could use when those on Earth run out.

✳ Humans will always search for knowledge. By studying our space "neighbourhood", we can learn more about how the Earth was formed and how life on Earth began. We must continue on the space exploration path – new opportunities and amazing discoveries could lie ahead.

Our future lies in space.

Seeing the invisible

For about 40 years, astronauts have been travelling into space to study the Universe, while astronomers have been studying the Universe for nearly 400 years, through telescopes. Although today's telescopes on Earth are very powerful instruments, their views are restricted by the **atmosphere**. To overcome this problem, many telescopes have been launched into space to **orbit** the Earth. From here they have a much clearer view.

Instead of recording visible light waves (the different colours we can see), many **satellite** telescopes have been designed to record other wavelengths in the **electromagnetic spectrum**. These are recorded as electronic signals, and the data is beamed down to Earth where computers turn it into visible images. These images have provided exciting information about otherwise invisible objects in space that are thousands of **light-years** away.

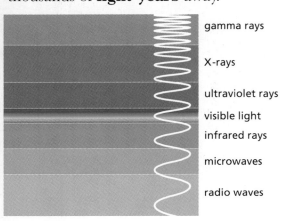

gamma rays

X-rays

ultraviolet rays

visible light

infrared rays

microwaves

radio waves

▲ The electromagnetic spectrum

Pathways to the invisible

Uhuru, launched 1970
Uhuru, the first X-ray satellite, recorded a detailed X-ray map of the sky. Later X-ray satellites discovered the remains of exploded **stars** and mysterious **quasars** that are 10,000 million light-years away!

Copernicus, launched 1972
Copernicus made the first ultraviolet observations from space. Ultraviolet radiation is given off by hot gas and by stars with temperatures of millions of degrees.

International Ultraviolet Explorer, launched 1978
One of the most successful satellites ever launched was the *International Ultraviolet Explorer.* It made thousands of ultraviolet light observations. It had been built to last three years, but in fact worked for 18!

▲ The *International Ultraviolet Explorer*

Infrared Astronomical Satellite (IRAS), 1983

IRAS only operated for nine months, but it picked up over 240,000 infrared sources in space. In 1995, the *Infrared Space Observatory (ISO)* was put into orbit. It has found evidence of the birth of stars and colliding **galaxies**.

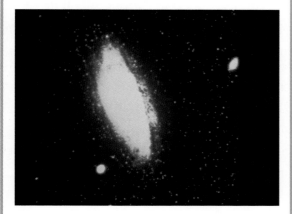

▲ Picture of Andromeda galaxy, taken by *ISO*

Cosmic Background Explorer (COBE), 1989

COBE was the first satellite telescope to pick up microwave data. It provided some clues as to how the Universe began (see page 27).

Compton Gamma Ray Observatory, 1991

This orbiting observatory picks up gamma rays. Gamma rays reveal details of some of the most fascinating objects and events in the Universe, such as **black holes** and **supernova** explosions.

Hubble Space Telescope (HST), 1990

The *Hubble Space Telescope* is the largest and most complex satellite ever built. It orbits over 600 km above Earth. The telescope has taken thousands of images of the Universe. In 1995, it made a ten-day study of one small part of space, but this gave enough information for teams of astronomers to study for years. The study is known as the Hubble Deep Field, and is believed to contain a history of the whole Universe as it records galaxies at every stage of their development.

▼ The *Hubble Space Telescope*

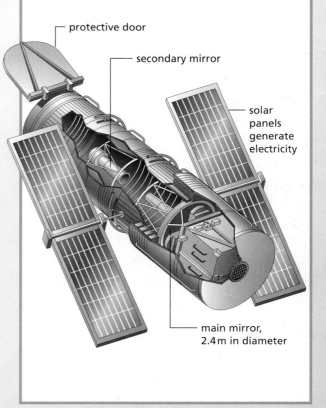

protective door

secondary mirror

solar panels generate electricity

main mirror, 2.4m in diameter

Robots in space

The Sun, nine **planets** and their **moons**, as well as **comets**, **meteors**, and **asteroids** make up the Solar System. To explore even our nearest neighbour (the Moon) using crewed flights alone would be too difficult, dangerous, and expensive.

Instead, **lunar** and interplanetary probes have been developed. Not all have been successful, but many have sent back photographs and other data from the Moon and from the planets. Here is a selection of successful probe missions to our nearest neighbours.

1966 *Luna 9:* soft-lander probe

The Russian *Luna 9* was the first craft to land successfully on the Moon. It took photographs of the Moon's rocky landscape and beamed them back to Earth. Its success removed fears that there were thick layers of dust on the Moon that would make future crew landings impossible.

▲ *Luna 9*

1970 *Luna 17:* lunar rover

Luna 17 took the first "robotic" rover to the Moon. Operated from Earth like a toy car, *Lunokhod 1* travelled 10.5 km across the Moon's surface, taking 20,000 photographs and **analyzing** rock samples.

1970 *Mariner 9:* Mars orbiter

The American *Mariner 9* was the first craft to **orbit** Mars. It took photographs that amazed astronomers. For example, it revealed volcanoes on Mars' surface. Among them was the vast Olympus Mons – three times the height of Everest, Earth's highest mountain.

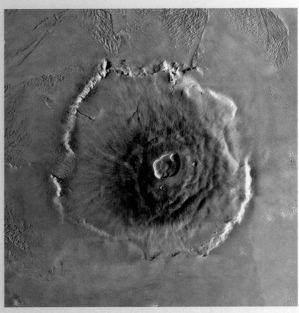

▲ A photograph of Olympus Mons on Mars, taken by *Mariner 9*

▼ A *Viking* lander on Mars

1974 *Mariner 10:* Mercury orbiter

Mariner 10 visited Mercury, the planet closest to the Sun. Its photographs showed a barren landscape pitted with craters. There were also mountains, cliffs, and plains.

1975 *Vikings 1* and *2:* Mars landers

These landers were sent to look for evidence of life on Mars. They took photographs of the rocky, red landscape and tested soil for living organisms, but no firm evidence of life was found.

1981 *Veneras 13* and *14:* Venus landers

Venus is closer to us than Mars but has long been a mystery because its surface is hidden by a dense, cloudy **atmosphere**. *Veneras 13* and *14* were the first probes to send back colour photos of the surface.

1997 *Pathfinder:* Mars rover

Balloons were inflated to cushion the landing of the Mars *Pathfinder*. The rover, called *Sojourner*, was driven down a ramp onto the Martian surface to analyze rocks and take more than 500 photographs.

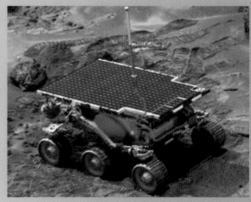

▲ *Sojourner* exploring the surface of Mars

2001 *NEAR Shoemaker*

The *Near Earth Asteroid Rendezvous* probe landed on an asteroid called Eros, 250 million km from Earth. It photographed and mapped the surface of this vast rock, 33 km in length.

Deeper into space

▼ This photograph of Jupiter's Great Red Spot was transmitted from *Voyager 2*.

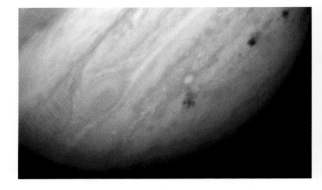

Beyond Mars lie four giant **planets** – Jupiter, Saturn, Uranus, and Neptune. The journeys to these planets take a long time, so robot space probes have been used to reach them. The most distant planet in our Solar System, Pluto, has not yet been reached, even by a probe.

Pioneers 10 and 11

Pioneer 10 began its 21-month journey to Jupiter in 1972. To reach Jupiter it had to pass through the **asteroid** belt, which is made up of billions of **orbiting** rocks. Scientists were worried that, if a large rock hit the craft, it would be destroyed. Fortunately, *Pioneer 10* and the probes that followed got through safely.

During *Pioneer's* Jupiter fly-by it took many photographs and helped to solve the mystery of Jupiter's "Great Red Spot". This permanent mark on Jupiter's surface was found to be a vast whirling storm. *Pioneer 10* continued on its path, leaving the Solar System in 1983 and heading for the **stars**. Signals from the craft are still picked up.

Pioneer 11 was launched in 1973. Like *Pioneer 10*, it took photographs of Jupiter and **analyzed** its **atmosphere**. It then went on to the first-ever mission to Saturn and took photographs of the planet's amazing rings.

Voyagers 1 and 2

Voyagers' multi-planet missions provided beautiful, detailed photographs of the giant outer planets. Both were launched in 1977. After following *Voyager 1* to Jupiter and Saturn, *Voyager 2* then went on to visit Uranus and Neptune.

The probes' photographs and data provided a mass of new knowledge about the planets and their **moons**. They discovered active volcanoes on Jupiter's moon, Io. While telescopes had shown nine moons round Saturn, the *Voyagers* found 18 there! Astronomers knew of five moons around Uranus, but *Voyager 2* found ten more, ranging in size from 160 km to less than 32 km in diameter.

▼ Saturn's rings

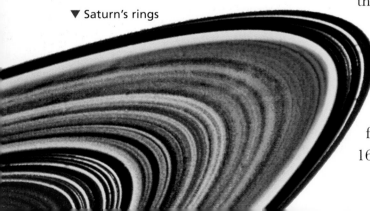

Voyager 2's fly-by of Neptune provided more details of its rings and atmosphere. Its last objective was to study Triton, one of Neptune's moons. Data from *Voyager 2* showed that, with a temperature of −235°C, Triton is the coldest known place in the Solar System. On the icy surface, there are frozen lakes, and geysers that shoot plumes of gas and ice into the atmosphere.

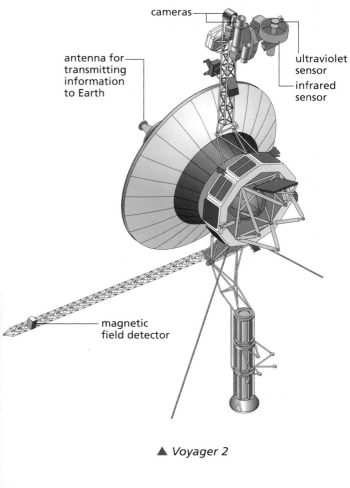

▲ *Voyager 2*

▼ As the *Voyager 2* probe flew by, it got a boost of energy from the **gravity** of each planet.

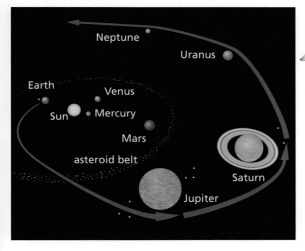

Probe	Launched	Destination
Giotto	1985	Reached Halley's **Comet** in 1986 – took photographs and data as it passed through the comet's gas and dust.
Galileo	1989	Reached Jupiter in 1995 – one section descended into the atmosphere (transmitted data for 57 minutes) while the other orbited Jupiter.
Magellan	1989	Reached Venus in 1990 and mapped the surface.

Space stations

Space stations stay in Earth's **orbit**, allowing plenty of time for astronomers and astronauts aboard to study the Earth below, and outer space. They also carry out experiments. Although the first space stations only stayed in orbit for a few months and then fell back to Earth, more recent space stations have remained in orbit for several years.

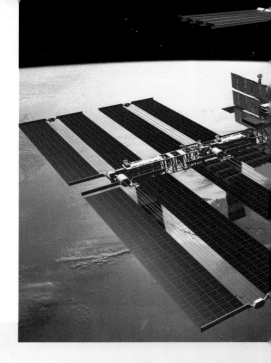

1971

The Soviet Union launched the first of its *Salyut* space stations. A three-man crew worked in it for 24 days, but disaster followed – the men died on re-entering the Earth's **atmosphere**. Later *Salyut* stations were very successful. Each had a docking section, workshop, living quarters, and a section containing the spacecraft's controls.

1973

The American *Skylab* space station was launched. Astronauts worked in the station for a total of 171 days. In 1979, the abandoned space station's orbit became too low, and the craft burnt up in the Earth's atmosphere.

▶ Shuttles take crew to and from *Mir*. Here is a view of the shuttle *Atlantis* closing in on *Mir*.

1986

The Soviet Union launched *Mir* in 1986. Several new sections were added later, including a 20-tonne laboratory. Although it was only designed to last for five years, extra money from the USA kept it going. In March 2001, *Mir* was closed down and sent into the Earth's atmosphere. Most of *Mir* burnt up before falling into the South Pacific.

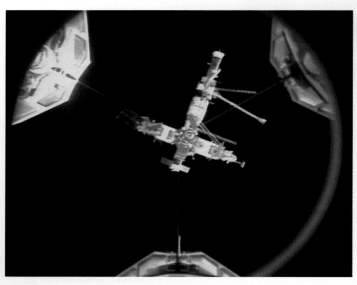

▲ The *International Space Station* (*ISS*) is both a research centre and a stepping stone for missions to the **Moon** and distant **planets**, such as Mars.

▲ To prevent his drink from floating away, astronaut James Voss floats about the *International Space Station* with a drink bag in his mouth.

▶ Astronauts must exercise regularly while in space to prevent their muscles wasting away.

International Space Station

This space station is currently being built in space and will take several years to complete. Its total cost is estimated at $35–37 billion. Several countries, including the USA, Russia, Canada, and Japan, are involved. The first of over 30 flights to take the pieces into space and nearly 40 additional missions to put them together have begun. The station includes living areas and laboratories, and is staffed permanently by crew.

Russian *Soyuz* spacecraft and US shuttles can **dock** to bring crew and supplies. Large solar panels use the Sun's power to provide electricity.

Weightlessness

Once the engines have been turned off, the crew in a space station or other spacecraft experience weightlessness. Because they are in free-falling orbit around the Earth they float around, along with any other objects that have not been tied down. To stay fit in these conditions, the crew have to exercise regularly.

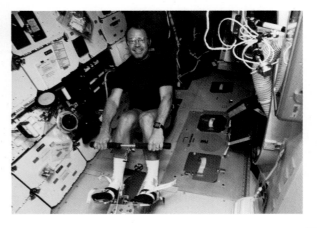

Looking for answers

Is there life out there?

Our Sun is one of many **stars** in the Universe – there are 100 billion stars in our **galaxy** alone, so perhaps there are more **planets** similar to our Earth. We have no evidence of other planets beyond our Solar System, but astronomers have spotted stars around which planets may be orbiting. Many people think there could be life on other planets; others think that a unique chain of events occurred to create life on Earth and that this chain of events is unlikely to have been repeated.

Life on Mars?

Some scientists think that shapes found in a Martian **meteorite** were the fossils of once-living Martian bacteria. This would prove that there had been living organisms on Mars. Other scientists are less certain and are still puzzling over the rock.

▼ *Voyagers 1* and *2* carried gold-plated audio-visual discs with sounds from Earth and scientific information – in case the probes come across intelligent life forms in outer space.

▲ This radio dish has sent a message to stars that are thousands of **light-years** away, in the hope that there is someone listening!

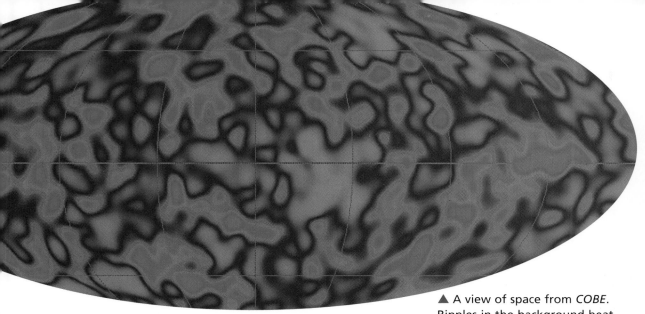

▲ A view of space from *COBE*. Ripples in the background heat radiation (the pink and red areas) are where the first stars and galaxies formed.

How did the Universe begin?

Many scientists believe that the Universe began with a "Big Bang" – a massive, hot explosion. In the 1920s, astronomers showed that the Universe is expanding, with all its galaxies and clusters of galaxies rushing apart. This expansion is thought to be the on-going result of the Big Bang explosion. In 1992, the *Cosmic Background Explorer* **satellite** (*COBE*) found new evidence of the Big Bang. Its data revealed background heat radiation caused by the explosion.

How was our galaxy formed?

In 1996, the *Hubble Space Telescope* recorded one small section of sky over ten days. The results, called the Hubble Deep Field, revealed at least 1500 galaxies. Because the galaxies are at different stages in their development, scientists can use this information to learn how galaxies, such as our own Milky Way, were formed.

▼ An image from the Hubble Deep Field

In the future

▲ The *VentureStar's* first flight is planned for 2015.

Amazing spacecraft

In the future, you might be able to take a trip to a space station in an aeroplane. New craft are always being considered. In the USA, the National Aeronautics and Space Administration (NASA) is already developing a "spaceplane" called the *VentureStar*. It is being designed specifically for taking passengers to the *International Space Station* and will replace the shuttle.

Future probes

Interplanetary probes will continue to discover the secrets of the Solar System. *Cassini*, launched in 1997, is currently heading for Saturn. It should arrive in 2004. Once in **orbit**, it will release a smaller probe, called *Huyghens*, to investigate Titan, one of Saturn's **moons**.

All spacecraft have so far used rocket power and fuel to travel. The amount of fuel needed to travel a long way makes a craft too heavy, so a new idea is going to be tested. In 2005, a spacecraft with a solar sail will use the power of solar wind. Solar wind is not like wind on Earth. Its force is a stream of atomic particles that flows out from the Sun at speeds of 300–1000 kph.

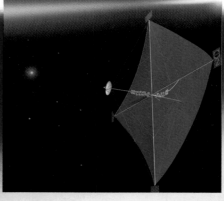

▲ A spacecraft with solar sails should fly through space like a kite.

▶ *Huyghens* should descend through Titan's atmosphere to land safely on the surface.

◀ Land modules for a Martian base, designed by NASA

Factories in space

In the future, complete factories may be built in space to orbit the Earth. Many items are made more easily in weightless conditions because of the way the materials behave in space. Large crystals, which can be used to make microchips for computers, can be grown more efficiently, and some new medicines may be manufactured more easily in space.

Moon and Martian bases

In the future, bases on the Moon or Mars may be built as stepping stones for missions to more distant **planets**. They could also house laboratories for astronomers and scientists. Giant telescopes built on the **Moon** would be effective as there is no **atmosphere** to restrict their view.

NASA has plans to eventually land astronauts on Mars. Land **modules** for a Martian base have also been designed. These will be similar to the modules that make up the *International Space Station*. Astronauts investigating the surface would look for minerals that could be worth mining.

Space junk

Space exploration has already left behind 150,000 large pieces of debris in Earth's orbit. These include old **satellites** and rocket parts. In 1999, a US satellite was launched to monitor the debris, and the *International Space Station* is being built with an extra covering to protect it from the debris – at an extra cost of $5 billion.

Planet facts

Key

- ● Name of planet
- ✲ Mean distance from Sun (millions of kilometres)
- 🚀 Year of first successful fly-by (spacecraft)

● Mercury
✲ 58
🚀 1973 (*Mariner 10*)

● Venus
✲ 108
🚀 1962 (*Mariner 2*)

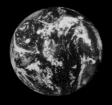

● Earth
✲ 150

● Mars
✲ 228
🚀 1965 (*Mariner 4*)

● Jupiter
✲ 779
🚀 1973 (*Pioneer 10*)

● Saturn
✲ 1427
🚀 1979 (*Pioneer 11*)

● Uranus
✲ 2869
🚀 1986 (*Voyager 2*)

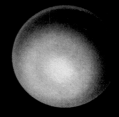

● Neptune
✲ 4496
🚀 1989 (*Voyager 2*)

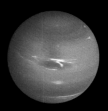

● Pluto
✲ 5899
🚀 not yet reached by probe

Glossary

analyze To look at and examine in detail.

asteroid A rocky object (also called a minor planet) that orbits the Sun. Most asteroids are in a belt between the orbits of Mars and Jupiter.

atmosphere The gases that surround a planet or moon.

black hole A region of space where matter is so dense nothing can escape from it – not even light.

capsule A detachable part of a spacecraft, which contains instruments. For example, the section in which astronauts land back on Earth.

comet An icy object surrounded by gas and dust which develops a tail of gas and dust as it approaches the Sun.

dock To join in space.

electromagnetic spectrum The complete range of wavelengths, from short to long, of electric and magnetic energy.

galaxy A vast system of stars, gas, and dust. Our Solar System is in the galaxy we call the Milky Way.

G-forces G-forces are experienced by astronauts and pilots when their craft rapidly speeds up or slows down. 1-G is the force of gravity on Earth; 20-G would crush a human body.

gravity A force that pulls, or attracts, one object to another. For example, gravity keeps us on the Earth's surface and the Earth in orbit around the Sun.

light-year The distance travelled by light in one year (9.3 billion km).

lunar To do with our Moon, or another moon.

meteor Particles of matter that are seen as a streak of light in the sky as they burn up in the Earth's atmosphere.

meteorite A rocky object that falls from space onto the surface of the Earth.

module A section of a spacecraft that can be detached.

moon A natural object that orbits a planet – for example, our Moon.

orbit The path a moon or spacecraft takes round a planet, or the path a planet takes round the Sun.

planet A natural object, such as the Earth, that orbits a star.

quasar A luminous object in space that may be the centre of a distant galaxy.

reflector A telescope that uses a mirror to gather light from the object being viewed.

refractor A telescope that uses a large lens to gather light, which a small eyepiece then magnifies.

satellite An artificial satellite is a manufactured spacecraft that orbits a planet; a natural satellite is a moon.

seismometer An instrument that detects and records earthquakes or "moonquakes".

star A globe of gases that emits heat and light (our Sun is a star).

supernova An explosion when a star is blown apart.

zero-gravity Weightlessness in space.

Books for further reading

Sean Connolly, *Heinemann Profiles: Neil Armstrong* (Heinemann Library, 1999)

Heather Couper and Nigel Henbest, *Big Bang, The Story of the Universe* (Dorling Kindersley, 1997)

Harry Ford, *The Young Astronomer* (Dorling Kindersley, 1998)

Eva M Hans, *Spinning through Space: Comets and Asteroids* (Hodder Wayland, 2001)

Nigel Hawkes, *The New Book of Mars* (Aladdin/Watts Books, 1998)

Jon Kirkwood, *Stars and Galaxies* (Franklin Watts Books, 1999)

Peter Mellett, *Launching a Satellite* (Heinemann Library, 1999)

Ian Ridpath, *Dorling Kindersley Handbooks, Stars and Planets* (Dorling Kindersley, 1998)

Index